POETRY Wonderland

Rhymes From Scotland

Edited By Sarah Olivo

First published in Great Britain in 2019 by:

YoungWriters®
Est. 1991

Young Writers
Remus House
Coltsfoot Drive
Peterborough
PE2 9BF
Telephone: 01733 890066
Website: www.youngwriters.co.uk

All Rights Reserved
Book Design by Spencer Hart
© Copyright Contributors 2019
SB ISBN 978-1-78988-488-3
Printed and bound in the UK by BookPrintingUK
Website: www.bookprintinguk.com
YB0404O

FOREWORD

Here at Young Writers, we love to let imaginations run wild and creativity go crazy. Our aim is to encourage young people to get their creative juices flowing and put pen to paper. Each competition is tailored to the relevant age group, hopefully giving each pupil the inspiration and incentive to create their own piece of creative writing, whether it's a poem or a short story. By allowing them to see their own work in print, we know their confidence and love for the written word will grow.

For our latest competition Poetry Wonderland, we invited primary school pupils to create wild and wonderful poems on any topic they liked – the only limits were the limits of their imagination! Using poetry as their magic wand, these young poets have conjured up worlds, creatures and situations that will amaze and astound or scare and startle! Using a variety of poetic forms of their own choosing, they have allowed us to get a glimpse into their vivid imaginations. We hope you enjoy wandering through the wonders of this book as much as we have.

CONTENTS

All Saints' Primary School, Airdrie

Sophia Phillips (7)	1
Orlaith Suzanne McMullen (7)	2
Heather Collins (7)	3
Mya McClenaghan (7)	4
Sienna Bryden (6)	5
Austin Docherty (7)	6
Marc Antony McDermott (7)	7
Gracie James Rowan (7)	8
Rhys Mullen (7)	9
Tristan Love (7)	10
Daniel Mullen (7)	11

Glenboig Primary School, Glenboig

Rosie Crilley (9)	12
Jayme-Leigh Mullen (10)	14
Lilly-Grace Barrett (10)	15
Mia Mcarthur (10)	16
Ebony-Jane Frances (9)	17
Ben McCutcheon (10)	18
Poppy Willow Robinson (10)	20
Heather Cole (8)	21
Matthew Joiner (10)	22
Thomas John Cockburn (9)	23
Josh Hartley (10)	24
Poppy Crilley (9)	25
Ben Kilfedder (9)	26
Lily Fulton (9)	27
Grace Shaw (9)	28
Catie Mcdonald (10)	29
Katee Hardman (9)	30
Callum Struzik (10)	31
Morgan Caillau (10)	32
Lewis Oattes (8)	33
Scott Wilson (11)	34
Adam Mullen (11)	35
Noah Godfrey (10)	36
Heather Brown (10)	37
Lilyann Davies (9)	38
Grace McNally (9)	39
Zoe McCutcheon (8)	40
Rhona Struzik (7)	41
Charlotte Godfrey (8)	42
Jayden Campbell (8)	43

Juniper Green Primary School, Edinburgh

Victor Alexander Ochnio (9)	44
Lisa Grace Neilson (8)	46
Caris Maia MacGregor-Duff (9)	48
Amy Louden	50
Charlie Stead	51
Sophie Brandligt (8)	52
Imogen Thomas (8)	53
Julia Hargreaves (8)	54
Charlotte Amy Clingan (8)	55
Cooper William Ward (10)	56
Emma Jane Banks (8)	57
Angus Veitch (8)	58
Lily Potter (9)	59
Lucy Smith (10)	60
Jacob Mackinnon (9)	61
Sofia Buell	62
Andrew Haddow (9)	63
Eva Graham	64
Lily Vinnicombe (8)	66
Anna Russell	67
Alex Cosmo Cochran	68

Alicia Harvey (9)	69
Aimie Victoria Burton (9)	70
Isla McClure (10), Rebekah Ralph & Emma	71
Evie Wong (8)	72
Lauren Ruby Kane (10)	73
Anum Dastagir (9)	74
Andrew Haddow (9)	75

Limekilns Primary School, Limekilns

Iona Young (9)	76
Liam Tait (8)	78
Aimee Alexander Lima (8)	79
Hannah Lauren Bayley (8)	80
Sienna McGee (8)	81
Phoebe Mason (8)	82
Emily Craig (8)	83
Ellie Stephen (8)	84
Jaimee Young (9)	85
Joshua Peacock (8)	86
Freya Byrne (9)	87
Louise McKay (9)	88
Rowan Grant (8)	89
Ernie Cruickshank (8)	90
Katie Mia Mulube (8)	91
Mason Smith (8)	92
Scarlet Donnelly (8)	93
Lucas Chaplin (8)	94
Connor Kevin Brady (8)	95
Rory Hastings (8)	96

Monymusk School, Monymusk

Anja Shepherd (8)	97
Matilda Esson (10)	98
Ashley Nicole Findlay (8)	99
Jack Strachan (9)	100
Shea Withey (9)	101
Lily Anne Chisholm (8)	102
Lily Emma Todd (9)	103
Reece Donaldson (7)	104
Michael Wood (7)	105

Zaysha Brand (8)	106
Andrew Mitchell (9)	107
Abby Ferguson (7)	108
Callum Reid (9)	109
Jake Peter Evans (7)	110

Newtongrange Primary School, Newtongrange

Teagan Sullivan (9)	111
Daisy Fiennes (9)	112
Flynn Dunlop (9)	115
Heather Breeze (9)	116
Vivienne Borkowska (9)	118
Ellie Macfarlane (9)	120
Jamie Ramsey (9)	122
Calla Meere (9)	124
Jennifer Aitken (9)	125
Kenzie O'Donnell (9)	126
Josh Jenkin (9)	127
Calum Higginson (9)	128
Eilidh Hill (9)	129
Alex Bell (9)	130
Thomas Hugh McSweeney (9)	131
Craig Dow (9)	132
Lilly Oldham (9)	133
Aila P Waite (9)	134
Aidan Byars (9)	135
Alana Moore (9)	136
Samuel Smith (9)	137
Iyla Croall (9)	138
Jack Smith (9)	139

Slains Primary School, Collieston

Hayley Dunn (11)	140
Stanley Sharp Grasham (11), Fraser Norrie, Brodie Macalister & Ollie Davidson (10)	142
Martha Crockett (11)	144
Maggie Cuthbert (10)	146
Esme Macalister (9)	148

Grace Bagshaw (11) & Piper Róisín Burrows	150
Ollie Davidson (10)	151

St Dominic's Primary School, Airdrie

Lewis Austin (11)	152
Cara Sweeney (11)	155
Olaf Filipiak (11)	156
Michael Fitzpatrick (11)	158
Alicja Matys (11)	160
Siobhan McGowan (11)	162
Taylor John McLaughlan (11)	164
Marvin Daly (11)	165
Shea McCarthy (11)	166
Chiara Reid (11)	167
Aiden Armstrong (11)	168
Aiden McGleish (11)	169
Fraser Courtney (11)	170
Jack Crawford (11)	171

Westerton Primary School, Bearsden

Neve Thompson (9)	172
Hayley Jessie Speedie (9)	174
Aimee Tabram (9)	175
Juliette Hay (9)	176
Murray Rasmussen (9)	178
Ethan MacPherson (9)	180
Phoebe Cuthbertson (9)	181
Suzie Rooney (9)	182
Tanisha Thapar (9)	183
Stuart MacKenzie (9)	184
Ava Mamie Wilson (10)	185
Isobel Collingwood (9)	186
Blair Auld (9)	187
Sophie Smith (9)	188
Anna McGregor (9)	189
Arya Chakraborty (8)	190
Euan Mitchell (10)	191
James Finch Mathew (9)	192
Lulu Alfayez (9)	193
Annie Miller (9)	194
Skye Dick (9)	195
Sophie Collins (9)	196
Anna White Wilson (10)	197
Lij McCulloch (9)	198
Oscar Murray Wilson (10)	199

The Poems

Guinea Pig Planet Adventure

My guinea pigs like to fly,
They decide to go to Planet Dye.
On Planet Dye,
They like to fly.
When they fly,
They both wear a tie.
The guinea pigs got a pie,
They ate the pie,
And said goodbye,
And they went to Planet Pie.
On Planet Pie,
They always said goodbye.
When they said goodbye,
They started to fly,
When they would fly, they'd eat a pie.
When they would eat the pie, they'd start to die.
When they'd die, they'd start to fly high,
They'd decide to say bye,
To go home before they started to die!

Sophia Phillips (7)
All Saints' Primary School, Airdrie

The Sweetie Planet

I once went out to space,
And ran at a lightning pace.
There were sweets everywhere,
There was even a chocolate sweet called Penny Pear.
I loved this planet best of all,
Because what other planets had sweets and all?
There were sweets of all kinds,
Some were disgusting, but the aliens didn't mind.
I have to say, this was the best trip of all,
And I remembered to sneak home one candy ball!

Orlaith Suzanne McMullen (7)
All Saints' Primary School, Airdrie

Rainbow Horses

R ainbow horses, munch, munch, munch.
A ngry rainbow horses, cross, cross, cross.
I n their stables, cosy, cosy, cosy.
N aughty rainbow horses steal, steal, steal.
B eautiful rainbow horses, clip, clip, clop.
O n rainbow horses it is fun, fun, fun.
W onderful rainbow horses, good, good, good.

Heather Collins (7)
All Saints' Primary School, Airdrie

Rainbow Bunny

R ainbow bunny hops, hops.
A ngry little bunny wants a carrot.
I nto the wood, hop, hop, hop.
N ow he wants to chomp, chomp, chomp.
B ouncing little bunny, bounce, bounce, bounce.
O h, wake up little bunny, sleep, sleep, sleep.
W ant a carrot, little bunny? Sleep, sleep, sleep.

Mya McClenaghan (7)
All Saints' Primary School, Airdrie

Flying Sausage Goes To Space

S ausage flies up in the sky,
A nd lands on the moon.
U p on the moon, he sings a tune,
S oon, the aliens give him a chase,
A way he runs at quite a fast pace!
G ets out of his hiding space in a rush,
E veryone tries to eat him, better stay hush!

Sienna Bryden (6)
All Saints' Primary School, Airdrie

The Sausage

Sing Sausage has lots of knowledge,
sing, sing, sing,
and he likes to swing, swing, swing.
You better run faster, little Sausage,
before you get caught!
Sausage has lots of little friends,
and they are all cooked,
and if one sausage is down,
they'll all have a frown!

Austin Docherty (7)
All Saints' Primary School, Airdrie

Dragons

D ragon with his cute little claws,
R ufus is his middle name,
A nd he likes lollipops.
G lad to play with the other dragons,
O ut of the forest they go,
N ow it's time to go home.
S leepy time for the dragons.

Marc Antony McDermott (7)
All Saints' Primary School, Airdrie

Unicorn

U nicorn wants to play.
N ow Unicorn wants to sleep, sleep, sleep.
I love Unicorn, she's so pretty!
C olours shine bright.
O h Unicorn, you beautiful thing.
R un free.
N ever look back.

Gracie James Rowan (7)
All Saints' Primary School, Airdrie

Lego Is Running Away

Lego everywhere, it starts to move,
Look at that one, it's in a groove.
It starts to run - oh look, it's away,
How will I get it back today?
They climb the stairs,
They do it in pairs.

Rhys Mullen (7)
All Saints' Primary School, Airdrie

Gummy Bears

Y ummy little gummy bears run,
U nder the bridge, through the town,
M iles and miles through the countryside,
M ummies chasing them!
Y ummy gummy bears gone for good.

Tristan Love (7)
All Saints' Primary School, Airdrie

Living Lego

L ittle Lego men are living now,
E ating their sausages, yum yum!
G ood Lego men, yay! Yay!
O ut of their houses they go, waving goodbye as they go.

Daniel Mullen (7)
All Saints' Primary School, Airdrie

Oh My Flower

Oh, my flower, oh, my flower
How you smell so sweet
Oh, my flower, oh, my flower
The bees that you will meet.

Oh, my flower, oh, my flower
As you dance in the summer's breeze
Oh, my flower, oh, my flower
The beauty that you seize.

Oh, my flower, oh, my flower
As the winter nears
Oh, my flower, oh, my flower
Time to shed some tears.

Oh, my flower, oh, my flower
As you slowly freeze
Oh, my flower, oh, my flower
Don't worry, spring comes with ease.

Oh, my flower, oh, my flower
As the ice will start to melt

Oh, my flower, oh, my flower
The joy that I have felt.

Oh, my flower, oh, my flower
How you smell so sweet
Oh, my flower, oh, my flower
The bees that you will meet.

Rosie Crilley (9)
Glenboig Primary School, Glenboig

The Genie

There was a genie who lived in a lamp,
She had a tiny wee lamb,
A girl called Kasey had a friend called Lacey,
They opened the lamp, there was a ramp,
It led down to the genie!
When they looked at the genie,
They thought she was quite teeny.

"Wow, you are a teeny, teeny genie!" said the girls,
When they finally saw the lamb,
They heard a big bang!
The ground started to shake,
They thought it was an earthquake,
Kacey started singing rhymes,
Lacey said it really wasn't the time!

While the earthquake started to stop,
They all looked shocked,
However, the genie said, "Do you want to go to the shops?"
They all agreed and skipped with no stops to the shops.

Jayme-Leigh Mullen (10)
Glenboig Primary School, Glenboig

Baxter Balloon

One day, there was a balloon called Baxter,
I watched it float in the morning breeze,
up above the rim of the window,
I thought it was a regular balloon, but suddenly a face appeared!

A crowd of people came around and started singing a lullaby rhyme,
"Baxter Balloon, Baxter Balloon, you came again,
To greet us with a morning blue."

As evening approached,
a wild range of people came again,
joined in, we all sang a rhyme together.
"Baxter Balloon, Baxter Balloon,
Fly up upon the moon
And come again soon."

Baxter Balloon was my friend,
and I hope to see him again,
it was an amazing adventure,
that came with a breathtaking view.

Lilly-Grace Barrett (10)
Glenboig Primary School, Glenboig

Pablo The Dog

The soft, smooth, furry dog slipped along a log,
The dog sat on a log that sat in a bog.
Suddenly, the log started to drop,
And the dog jumped off.

The dog slipped smoothly onto the floor and into a door,
The door slipped slowly open and the dog slipped in,
Behind the door was a door, the dog was curious.
Suddenly, there was a magic portal,
The portal asked the dog to say,
"Smooth, furry dog as soft as a pom-pom,
Go back in time, this is your time to shine."

The dog decided to go back in time,
So he said the words,
"Smooth, furry dog as soft as a pom-pom,
Go back in time, this is your time to shine!"

Mia Mcarthur (10)
Glenboig Primary School, Glenboig

The Dangerous Drapuppy

One boring afternoon, I was walking my pet Oppey,
Hurryingly, he pulled me off my feet because he saw a treat with lots of meat,
No one was around, not even a little sound,
Until Oppey sprinted down the quiet town,
The chiming clock passed an hour,
Oppey's coat was grey as cement,
Not the usual gold, shiny colour.
We got home, the house smelt wonderful,
Until Oppey walked in,
Suddenly, he stood on a pin,
Cautiously, I turned around, trying to walk away,
To try and save myself,
He blew and blew,
Burning the house down with anger,
We still love him just as much as that pin.

Ebony-Jane Frances (9)
Glenboig Primary School, Glenboig

Ready, Steady, Jump

There was a ball called Paul,
Who was not any good at basketball,
He was only good,
At being a dude.

In the hall, there was only one ball,
Because Jimmy had them all,
So Stephen took Paul,
And gave it his all.

He missed the shot,
Because of a pot,
It was in his way,
And there to stay.

So Paul the ball made a giant leap to the beat,
Using his sweet feet,
He went up high, higher than ever,
Doing the best dunk ever.

Stephen was given a big applause,
Even though he asked for a pause,

He was now the biggest hero,
Even though he started from zero!

Ben McCutcheon (10)
Glenboig Primary School, Glenboig

A Bluebird's Wing

One day, I looked out the window,
And I saw a bluebird fly away,
I watched it fly to a tree nearby,
And fly back to the window.

I saw the bird again today,
It flew to a bundle of sticks in a tree,
At first, I thought it was a mess,
Then I noticed it was a nest.

The next day, I noticed eggs in the nest,
The bluebird flew around the tree,
It landed in the nest,
And kept the eggs warm.

One day, I looked out the window,
And I saw four bluebirds fly away,
I watched them fly to a tree nearby,
And wondered,
Have those eggs hatched?

Poppy Willow Robinson (10)
Glenboig Primary School, Glenboig

A Sugar Rush

Candy Land was as sweet as sugar,
It had clouds of cotton candy.
Sugar (my pet dragon) and I had fun every day,
Sugar had the most glossy scales made of gummy strawberries,
But there was one thing...
She gave you big sugar rushes!
She blew fizzy drinks with extra sugar,
And you would get a sugar rush for a whole two weeks!
We bounced like frogs on the colourful clouds,
Suddenly, Sugar saw a talking marshmallow,
So she got frightened and gave it a sugar rush!
He sprinted away into a yummy cave.
Feeling tired like a child,
We flew off into the dark.

Heather Cole (8)
Glenboig Primary School, Glenboig

Food Planet

The food planet was food and all
But wasn't much like a ball

The chocolate sector had skyscrapers tall
Only chocolate could be bought at a shopping mall
The chocolate was very fine
But the people looked undivine

The burger part was very nice
It was so hot, there was no ice
People made burgers far and wide
Burgers stacked so high you could always hide

The Italian bit was very bright
Because food was cooking day and night

If you want to come here now
There's no point, 'cause the only food is a bit of cow.

Matthew Joiner (10)
Glenboig Primary School, Glenboig

My Dream Life

I wish my life was like this,
Yes, I wish, I wish, I wish,
That I was free, as free as a bird,
I wish my life was like this,
I wish, I wish, I wish.

I wish everything was sweets,
Except my bird called Tweets.
I wish my carpet was a Refresher that never went hard,
My house a great gingerbread man that walked and talked.

My cats would be big M&M's,
With cute little gummy bear ears,
If you ate them, you'd be ill,
And you would create tears.
I'd never need to pay my bills,
Because they're never filled.

Thomas John Cockburn (9)
Glenboig Primary School, Glenboig

The Football Explosion!

He stands over the free kick,
As the opposition's fans start to be sick.
The ball flying through the air,
Almost taking off people's hair!

The ball catches fire,
The pitch is dire,
Allianz Arena is just flames and rubble,
Everyone in the stadium is in trouble!

The fire brigade come,
But they can't help some.
Sirens blasting,
But the fire's still lasting.

The fire has stopped,
But friends and family have dropped.
The stadium is nothing but brick,
As people get really sick.

Josh Hartley (10)
Glenboig Primary School, Glenboig

Fly Away

Dragon, dragon, fly away, dragon,
Ride on a lightning bolt,
Dragon, dragon, keep on flying through that summer air,
Scaly, scary, happy dragon, ride on that lightning bolt!
Soar through the air like a happy bear,
Fly away, fly away, dragon!

Fairy, fairy, fly away, fairy,
Eat up your marmalade,
Fairies, fairies, you smell of daisies,
All on a summer's day.

Zombies, zombies, go away, zombies,
Nobody wants you here.
Zombies, zombies, horrible zombies,
Everyone's scared of you!

Poppy Crilley (9)
Glenboig Primary School, Glenboig

Slithery Snake

Slithery Snake as slim as a stick,
Slither your way back in time,
Slithery Snake, it's your time to pick,
Will you go back in time?

The slimy, soft, scaly snake,
Slowly slithered up the spiky, soft tree,
Slithery Snake, how will you get down?
Sami the owl slowly swooped the slithery snake quickly away to safety.

Slimy Snake said to Slithery Snake,
"Small, slimy, scaly, slim snake,
This is your time to go back in time again,
Fix your mistakes,
And you will shine again."

Ben Kilfedder (9)
Glenboig Primary School, Glenboig

Fly Away To Safety!

Fly away, fly away, fly away, my dragon,
Fly high into the sky,
Before the raging wind swoops you up into the burning fire!

Oh, fly higher, oh, fly higher,
Trust me this one time,
Go to the Lord of Wings,
And he will help you save the day.

Oh, my dragon, oh, my dragon, you saved the day!
I am so proud of you, my dragon,
For trusting me today!

I hope you learned your lesson,
That it is not so bad,
To trust someone on a needed day,
Fly away, fly away, fly away, my dragon!

Lily Fulton (9)
Glenboig Primary School, Glenboig

Butterfly, Butterfly

Butterfly, butterfly, fly so high,
your wings will guide you through the sky!
I will help you fly like a bird in the sky,
you will fly very high, try to fly so, so high.

Butterfly, butterfly, spread your wings,
through the wind, you'll hear birds sing,
flutter those beautiful red wings,
and so spring begins.

Butterfly, butterfly, swoop through the trees,
don't forget, look out for the bees!
You'll see the flowers dancing in the wind,
flowers are almost like friends.

Grace Shaw (9)
Glenboig Primary School, Glenboig

Cruel Hannah

There was a girl called Hannah,
She usually slipped on bananas,
Even when she was jumping,
Everything was thumping.

She had bananas in school,
And she thought she was rather cool,
And liked to play pool,
But she was really, really cruel.

All the girls screamed,
When she took their ice creams,
They all had a fit,
When Hannah took a bit.

When Hannah got home,
She asked for a gnome,
Suddenly, the girls came round,
And gave her a pound.

Catie Mcdonald (10)
Glenboig Primary School, Glenboig

A Dangerous Pet

One sunny afternoon, I went to check on Nessie,
But soon, I could hear quiet splashes like a mouse's footsteps.
I could see blue scales like the water floating.
Next, I could smell fresh air coming from the trees,
It was like a little breeze.
I could feel teeny tiny bits of water on my hands,
And finally, I could taste my dry mouth,
Whilst wondering where he was.
Interestingly, I heard a giant splash!
Then he came out saying, "Hello!"

Katee Hardman (9)
Glenboig Primary School, Glenboig

In The Blue

One day when I was at the beach
I saw a weird shape pop out the water
I thought it was a shark, but it was too close to shore
I grabbed a boat and whizzed out to sea

There were dolphins as joyful as summer!
I dived in
The dolphins were as fast as motorcycles
I fed them some fish, they gobbled it up.

I love dolphins, I took them back to shore
And showed them to my mum.
Me and my sister swam with them
For hours and hours.

Callum Struzik (10)
Glenboig Primary School, Glenboig

Far Away

Far away, far away,
How I see you shimmer.
You're like a star up in the sky,
Although a little bit dimmer.

Far away, far away,
There is where you lie,
Down below on the floor,
I sometimes hear your cry.

Far away, far away,
An enchanted castle lay,
Far away, far away,
The sun shines every day.

Far away, far away,
I'll come up today.
I'll fly from the bay,
Right under where you lay.

Morgan Caillau (10)
Glenboig Primary School, Glenboig

A Mythical Pet

One perishing afternoon, I was in the Arctic.
I heard terrifying howling,
It was as loud as a lion!
I strolled over to the noise in the distance,
I saw snow as white as a sheep's woolly coat.
Suddenly, I saw something as blue as the sky,
It approached me, it was a frozen dog,
Its name was Remus,
I felt stunned!
It was as cold as ice,
It was as shiny as a gem and
Its eyes were as light as the sun...

Lewis Oattes (8)
Glenboig Primary School, Glenboig

The Burger King

I was walking down the street
Then I noticed something on my feet
It was a new burger place planning sheet.

When I walked there, what I saw
Was the Burger King trying to withdraw
He broke the law
Because he didn't wear his claw.

He got arrested when his wife was in bed
In a shed.
I went to visit the king
But he was all the way in Kingtucky
A newly discovered country.

Scott Wilson (11)
Glenboig Primary School, Glenboig

The Devil's Angel

He stood there confused, "How will this work?"
The Devil was an angel and was ready to lurk.
He began to feel weird
It was clear to say
His good side had appeared
Just for a day.

It seemed Alice Angel had done it again
Ruining the Devil's fun, when would it end?
"Not until he is flushed down the drain!" she did say
Once again, Alice Angel saved the day.

Adam Mullen (11)
Glenboig Primary School, Glenboig

Hippogriff Fly

Hippogriff, hippogriff, flying high
Zooming through the summer sky
In the air, your wings will glide you up and up
Through the clouds in the blue
The sky is shining bright for you.

Who knows what you'll see
When you're up in the bright blue sky
Up high
You will fly
In the bright blue sky.

Through the wind, you will fly
Up and up through the sky.

Noah Godfrey (10)
Glenboig Primary School, Glenboig

Running With Dolphins

Their fins were flapping
as they ran across
the sand.
I had a banana
in my hand.

The banana fell
and no one could tell
until one of the dolphins slid
into an unfortunate skid.

The dolphin got up
and I gave him a
cup of tea
then he went
back to sea.

Heather Brown (10)
Glenboig Primary School, Glenboig

Rainbow Water

At the rainbow water
It gets even hotter
Going for a dive
Hoping I come out alive
I see a shark
That is very dark
I hit it on the nose
But it bites my toes
I swim away
The shark is looking for prey
Then I go for a drive
My mum eats me alive!

Lilyann Davies (9)
Glenboig Primary School, Glenboig

Chocolate Water

In the chocolate water
it got even hotter.
With candy canes
and chocolate lion manes.
I was going for a dive
hoping to come out alive.
I jumped out and went for a drive
and accidentally hit a hive.
I hit it with a log
and it turned into a frog!

Grace McNally (9)
Glenboig Primary School, Glenboig

Rainbow Water

Under the rainbow water
I got hotter and hotter
I was going for a dive
I was not alive
But I wanted to do the jive
On a beehive
So I came alive
And did another jive
On a beehive.

Zoe McCutcheon (8)
Glenboig Primary School, Glenboig

A Dragon In A House

A dragon in a house
was cooking a mouse.
After she cooked
she looked
at a gingerbread man.

Then a human came!
The dragon breathed fire
then he flew higher.

Rhona Struzik (7)
Glenboig Primary School, Glenboig

Rainbow Water

At the rainbow water
It gets even hotter
Going for a dive
Hoping to stay alive
Going for a drive
I see a beehive
I hit it with a stick
Then the bees get sick.

Charlotte Godfrey (8)
Glenboig Primary School, Glenboig

Party On The Moon

There was a party,
there was a big spoon,
it was for the jelly,
now it's in my belly.

Jayden Campbell (8)
Glenboig Primary School, Glenboig

My Family Poem

My dad is a bit lazy
I wish he could be a bit more crazy.
He's always watching TV
and that annoys me.
I wish he could spend more time with me
even though he does sometimes.
Tomorrow, I'm going to turn off the electricity
so he can't watch TV!

My sister is cute, but sometimes she
jumps out and annoys me like a bee!
She sounds like a squealing hyena.
Yesterday, she couldn't sleep
it was the worst day of my life!

My mum is always happy
and I mean always happy and busy.
She is always happy no matter what.
True fact: I hardly ever see her
she's always busy doing something.

I am crazy
I mean crazy like a daisy.

I'm always busy doing something
I wish I stopped being busy for a moment.
Tomorrow, I'm going to have a break.

Victor Alexander Ochnio (9)
Juniper Green Primary School, Edinburgh

My Family

My brother Noah loves gaming
he also loves sleep
he could do it all day
because he sleeps very deep.

My sister Beth is a waitress at Pizza Hut
she's always funny
and she's got pink hair too.

My mum is friendly and very happy too
almost all the time
she's very sporty
and loves to go out on a run.

My guinea pig Harry is always jumping
he's like a rabbit, jumpy and fun
he's like a big, furry hamster, happy and hungry.

My guinea pig Ron isn't that fluffy
he's sort of like a gerbil
because of his appetite.

My dad likes to sleep
he sometimes snores

but that's okay with me
'cause I sleep next door.

Lisa Grace Neilson (8)
Juniper Green Primary School, Edinburgh

Robin In The Snow

Robin robin red breast
in the cold, cruel snow
soaring and swooping
high in the sky.
The swishing wind takes you
faster and faster
as you get higher and higher.

Robin robin red breast
watch as you go
the wind takes you
where you don't want to go.
Tumbling, fluttering and falling from the sky
a damaged wing finds you furled
and curled on the captain's boat.

Robin robin red breast
how lucky have you been?
A kind, caring gentleman helps you at the scene.
You are mended
you are fixed
you are ready to go!

New adventures await you
and home do you go.

Caris Maia MacGregor-Duff (9)
Juniper Green Primary School, Edinburgh

My Family

My mum is so busy as a busy bee,
She is always running after the family,
She is always so beautiful as can be.

My dad is as silly as can be,
He sounds like a broken set of false teeth,
Yesterday, he was pranking me like the prankster he is.

I wish Ollie would stop dropping his ball,
Down the back of the settee.
My dog Ollie is really annoying,
We are always running after him,
But I still love him like the rest of the family.

My sister is the royal pest,
She is like a panda getting dressed!
My sister is always in her room, making a mess,
But I still love her like the rest of the family.

Amy Louden
Juniper Green Primary School, Edinburgh

My Family

My mum is really kind.
She always shouts like a bull.
She is like a busy bee.

My dad is lazy, I wish he was a bit crazy.
He always comes home from work and watches TV.
Yesterday, he drank seventeen cans of beer!

My big brother Liam is really annoying.
He never lets me go in goal in football.
He is very small for his age.
Sometimes, I wish I could go in goal
And be like him, never let him in goal.

My little sister Ava is crazy!
I like how she is not lazy.
I wish she wouldn't annoy me
And annoy my brothers instead.
If she did it, I would give her £100!

Charlie Stead
Juniper Green Primary School, Edinburgh

My Family

My mum is as loving as Cupid (not the reindeer),
She helps me tidy my room.
Sometimes I call her Dory
Because she's forgetful.

My dog Bruno is as crazy as me for food!
When you pet him,
He likes to put his back to you.
He sounds like all the Simpsons arguing when he barks.

My cat Misty is really lazy
And sleeps all the time, especially in the day.
She's really ill and could die soon,
But she still leaps off my bed a lot.

My gran is really kind,
She is as funny as a comedian.
Gran is helpful,
When you're hurt, she tries her best to help you.

Sophie Brandligt (8)
Juniper Green Primary School, Edinburgh

My Family

My brother is as cheeky as a monkey,
He is wound up easily as a jack-in-the-box,
Sometimes, I think he is a living devil!

My sister is sheep obsessed,
She is like a miniature teenager,
90% is her tiredness level.

My dad is clean and sometimes bossy,
He is like a giant ironing machine,
Dad reads me a lot of Harry Potter.

My mum is always as busy as a bee,
Going to work, taking us to school,
She's a bit like a lovely, lively otter.

You might think my family's worse than a ghost,
But me?
Well, I'm perfect (well, almost).

Imogen Thomas (8)
Juniper Green Primary School, Edinburgh

My Family!

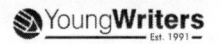

My sister is so annoying, but sometimes kind
She is always commenting on what I do
With my ever so magical mind
She is like a parrot to me!

My mum is sometimes boring
Sometimes as jolly as holly
Sometimes she lets me eat a lolly
Yesterday, she ate a carrot and had tea

My dad is a ton of fun
He likes a burger in a bun
When we go on rides together
I say, "Whee!"

My grandpa is lazy
I wish he could be more crazy
Tomorrow, I'll take him surfing
And he'll be free!!!

Julia Hargreaves (8)
Juniper Green Primary School, Edinburgh

My Family!

My mum is as busy as a bee
she always is working hard.
Sometimes, I wish she'd work less to see me.

My dad is tired out roaring at Grace.
Yesterday, he picked me up for school
I wish he would take a lie down.

Rebecca is really cheeky
she is like a cheeky monkey.
Tomorrow, I am going to tell her she is not my roomie.

Grace is really annoying
she is like a wasp buzzing in your ear.
Yesterday, she hugged me so tight
but I was still breathing.

I wish I could be alone for a while.

Charlotte Amy Clingan (8)
Juniper Green Primary School, Edinburgh

Football

- **F** un football, that's the way we play.
- **O** utstanding play every day.
- **O** verhead kick, smashing the net, then celebrating like a pet.
- **T** ackle of the century, goal of the decade.
- **B** allon d'Or for the best in the world, World Cup for the best country.
- **A** wesome skills, epic talents, they will never get tackled or lose their balance.
- **L** egs tired after ninety minutes.
- **L** osers after all of your hard work, unlucky people.

Cooper William Ward (10)
Juniper Green Primary School, Edinburgh

My Family!

My sister is sooo annoying
She always annoys me
She is as annoying as the sound of a buzzing bee.

My brother is like a gamer (he loves Fortnite)
He sounds like a lion during the night
He always picks me up for a fight!

My cat, well, she comes into your room
At six in the morning, meowing for food
She is soft and cute, but can scratch you real good.

And finally, my mum
She is perfect
Best of the best, better than the rest.

Emma Jane Banks (8)
Juniper Green Primary School, Edinburgh

My Family

My mum likes cooking
and she likes walking
going on holiday, relaxing
and watching TV.

My brother is as tall as a giraffe
and goes to work
he's sporty and goes with his friends
and I see him sometimes.

My dad is lazy
and goes swimming with me
and takes me to golf
and he's old and slow.

My cousin likes to play his iPad
and likes to play with his dog
and plays with Lego
and likes to go outside.

Angus Veitch (8)
Juniper Green Primary School, Edinburgh

Joy

Joy is building
in my bones.
It's a feeling I've
always known.
Jokes make me laugh
build a happiness path.
Smiles are so warm
they could break through a thorn
or cut through a storm.
Oh, smiles are
so warm.
As the sun rises above you
you call, "Woohoo!"
You're feeling happiness
in your head
you will feel it until you go to bed.
Joy makes me free
I scream, "Yippee!"

Lily Potter (9)
Juniper Green Primary School, Edinburgh

Red Robin, Red Robin Out In The Snow

Little red robin out one day
to get some nuts and maybe play.

Little red robin with the red breast
and the brown tummy in a brown dress
with a yellow golden beak, it makes him the best.

As happy as can be
he has a high-pitched squeak.

Mum says, "What took you so long,
my little robin boy?"

"I found a home not far from the ground
with berries and nuts all around."

Lucy Smith (10)
Juniper Green Primary School, Edinburgh

A Broken Heart

I wish you could feel my pain,
When I'm walking in the rain.
Feeling all by myself,
Since you left me,
I would very much rather,
Be stung by a bee.
It is over between us,
And stay away from each other we must.
Every time I think about you,
I feel so much woe,
And then I try to remember,
Why'd you go?
I knew there was a price to pay,
Now there's just one thing to say,
Goodbye.

Jacob Mackinnon (9)
Juniper Green Primary School, Edinburgh

Elephants

E motional elephants are always elegant,
L ovely, long, loud elephants lounging in mud,
E verything exciting, never boring,
P erfect performances, people are proud,
H appy elephants hunted 'til death,
A mazing elephants, angry poachers,
N aughty people destroying habitats,
T all trees, tied and pulled down,
S mall elephants, sad, scared and lonely.

Sofia Buell
Juniper Green Primary School, Edinburgh

Off On A Trip

The sweet sounding robin with its little red belly
passes by, gracefully flying
landing to nibble at a nut
then back on its feet.
Fly, fly, quick, quick
fly fast, don't stop
I see in your big brown eyes that you want to keep going.
Oh no! Thunder, fly low!
Hide!
Back home, we go back
cuddle in, get warm
come some other day to play.

Andrew Haddow (9)
Juniper Green Primary School, Edinburgh

Robin, Robin

Robin, robin
in the sky
Robin, robin
loves to fly
Robin, robin
up so high
Robin, robin
up and down
Robin, robin
all around
Robin, robin
here and there
Robin, robin
is so merry
Robin, robin
flies so steady
Robin, robin
is so ready
so
Robin, robin
off you go

Robin, robin
fly home.

Eva Graham
Juniper Green Primary School, Edinburgh

My Family

My mummy is kind as the girl next door
we play and play
until we hear my dad snore.

My daddy likes football
winning is his aim
and football is his game.

My sister is like a world famous gymnast
and famous people go wild for her.

My puppy is fluffy, funny and friendly
he makes other dogs laugh
and he is loud as thunder.

Lily Vinnicombe (8)
Juniper Green Primary School, Edinburgh

My Family

My dad is quite funny,
he likes a run,
after he's run, he likes a coffee.

My mum loves cleaning,
she loves a board game,
yesterday, she was helpful and happy.

My cousin loves hockey,
she is so active,
she loves every sport.

My uncle loves a marathon,
he always is fun,
yesterday, he was as fast as a cheetah.

Anna Russell
Juniper Green Primary School, Edinburgh

The Monster In The Wood

He wallows in the darkness
and he drowns in his tears.
He screams in the dark
for all to hear.
Oh, how he wishes for love,
but who would love a monster?
Scared his friends away
with a single hideous glare.
How would one ever enter his shame?
He stays in the distance and stares
for who would have a monster as a friend?

Alex Cosmo Cochran
Juniper Green Primary School, Edinburgh

Unicorns

Unicorns are pink
Unicorns are magical.

Flying high above the sky
Dancing through rainbows.

Unicorns are glittery and pink
If you saw a unicorn, what would you think?

I believe in unicorns
They believe in me.

If I saw a unicorn
I'd scream out, "Yippee!"

Alicia Harvey (9)
Juniper Green Primary School, Edinburgh

Robin, Robin

Robin, robin
up so high
robin, robin
all so fast
robin, robin
wet and cold
robin, robin
in the sky
robin, robin
warm at home
robin, robin
fly solo
robin, robin
flying through the sky
robin, robin
looking for nuts
robin, robin
flying through the snow.

Aimie Victoria Burton (9)
Juniper Green Primary School, Edinburgh

Robin, Robin

Robin, robin
looks so red
Robin, robin
look ahead

Robin, robin
look up high
Robin, robin
in the sky

Robin, robin
twirl around
Robin, robin
touch the ground

Robin, robin
red breast
Robin, robin
rest.

Isla McClure (10), Rebekah Ralph & Emma
Juniper Green Primary School, Edinburgh

My Family

My sister is as funny as a lizard
and she eats like a pig

My daddy is as sleepy as a bear
and playful as a dog

My cat's moany as a bear
and she is so fluffy

My mum is careful as a doctor
and she loves to read.

Evie Wong (8)
Juniper Green Primary School, Edinburgh

Robin, Robin

Robin, robin is so grey
Robin, robin lands on hay
Robin, robin, who flew and fled
Robin, robin, with his chest so red
Robin, robin, all alone
Robin, robin is now at home.

Lauren Ruby Kane (10)
Juniper Green Primary School, Edinburgh

Winter

W arm PJs, nice and cosy
I ce skating fun
N ever warm
T eddy, cosy
E lf, amazing!
R ainy water.

Anum Dastagir (9)
Juniper Green Primary School, Edinburgh

Music, Music

Music, music
sounds so sweet
music, music
has a beat
music, music
is not bad
music, music
is so rad!

Andrew Haddow (9)
Juniper Green Primary School, Edinburgh

Cake Land

The people here in Cake Land
they're just like you and me
they have their breakfast, eat their lunch
but all have cake for tea.

Cake Land is amazing,
you'll always have some fun
the children here are friendly
and play with everyone.

The beds are made from cupcakes
with icing for the sheet
the pillows made of mallow
that children sometimes eat!

The cook is very busy
making batter every day
with eggs and flour and sugar...
but oops, no butter to weigh!

She looks around the kitchen
for something else to use

and then she sees a bowl of fruit
with healthy things to choose.

Cake Land's still a happy place
with lots of things to eat
but now the kids are fit and strong
and cakes are just a treat!

Iona Young (9)
Limekilns Primary School, Limekilns

Monster School

M onsters stomping through the corridor
"O h no! A human! Argh!
N o, there are hundreds of them!"
"S top right where you are, monsters!"
"T he humans are coming in! Oh no! What should we do?
E gghead, we need you!" "I will be right down
R ight, where are you, monsters? Come out, come out!"

S chool, are you ready to rumble?
C harge! The fight has begun!
"H o ho ho!" Oh no! It is the evil Santa! Run!
O n the way to the town, the three-headed dog gets shot
O n the way to one of the shops in the town, the skeleton gets shot
L ook, here comes Egghead! "Hi, Egghead!"

Liam Tait (8)
Limekilns Primary School, Limekilns

Upside-Down Brazil

U pside-down Brazil is the best
P eople watch flying eels soar
S ky surfing is my thing
I n the ice-cold water, crazy people go
D o a little dance and prance
E lectric waves through the air

D own to the sea floor they go
O ver the dusty rocks
"W ow!" they all say
N o one knows what to do but sit and stare

B rick sand we walk across
R ed blood rain is what falls
A fter all that, I'll take you away
Z oos are amazing in a backwards land
I slands don't exist at all, anyway
L ike all good things, it must finally end.

Aimee Alexander Lima (8)
Limekilns Primary School, Limekilns

Can You Imagine If Elephants Lived In Space?

C razy elephant
R acing to the moon
A stronauts float by, so the elephant gives them a wave
Z ingy zingy mocktails are coming from space
Y ay! Whee! Whoosh!

E verywhere is so open for elephants to spin and turn
L ater on, there's going to be a big space storm
E ven if I could do anything, I would live in space
P hones would not exist if I lived in space
H unting things with all my friends
A ll peaceful in outer space
N ever annoy an elephant floating in a galaxy
T his is the crazy elephant.

Hannah Lauren Bayley (8)
Limekilns Primary School, Limekilns

Party On The Sun

Parties are so much fun
especially when you're dancing on the sun.
I see the moon from miles away
it's so rocky today.
Let's invite people to the sun
to have some fun.
The dancefloor is so bright
I think people can see us tonight.
The galaxy is so nice
I'm glad I had a party tonight!
An astronaut stops by to take a balloon
for his journey to the moon.
Now the party's nearly done
hand out the cake to the people that had some fun.

Sienna McGee (8)
Limekilns Primary School, Limekilns

Animal Land

A nimal Land is amazing
N o, it is not scary
I n the jungle, you can see elephant trunk slides
M onkeys are swinging from the trees
A wesome apes peeling bananas
L ions are snoring all night, silently, their manes swaying as time goes past

L eaping leopards are jumping away
A nts are all over the ground
N earby, cheetahs are racing up and down
D irty animals are washing in the river.

Phoebe Mason (8)
Limekilns Primary School, Limekilns

Starbucks

S tars were everywhere
T he stars were even falling from the ceiling
"A re you ready to pay for all your Starbucks?"
"R eady as I'll ever be," I said
B *oom!* As a horse appeared outside, hurting everyone
U nbelievably, unicorns were flying everywhere
"C an you guys see them?" I asked
K oalas were entering the door, my day was so fun!
S tarbucks is amazing!

Emily Craig (8)
Limekilns Primary School, Limekilns

Crazy Land

C razy Land is so much fun!
R ide the car round and round
A mazing doughnuts having fun
Z ipping, sliding on the ice
Y odelling doughnuts on the hill

L and is fading, let's sit round the doughnut sunset
A round people come with little marshmallows
N ow time to sleep on our marshmallow pillows
D ay has come, Gummy Cat is here! Jelly Dog is having fun.

Ellie Stephen (8)
Limekilns Primary School, Limekilns

My Trip To Space

I pack my case
to go to space
I empty my pocket
to get in my rocket
the space school
is cool
everything in the classroom floats
and we are trying to make boats
I make friends with an alien called Summer
and she is the fastest floating runner
but now the day is done
it's time to go, it's been fun
so let's empty my pocket
to get in my rocket.

Jaimee Young (9)
Limekilns Primary School, Limekilns

Cappy Meets A Tornado

In the Cap Kingdom, far away
Cappy was on a thin ledge.
Argh! He fell off the edge!
Cappy teleported somewhere,
Somewhere new out there.
Someone else was there too,
But then... he made a tornado!
Cappy needed to find a head,
At last, he got a head!
Then he said, "Now, throw me at that dusty-looking dread!"
Then they shouted, "We won! We won!"

Joshua Peacock (8)
Limekilns Primary School, Limekilns

Cupcake Crazy

I live inside a cupcake
Bang! Up goes another popping candy explosion
Get ready to catch it
Jump!
Dripping yummy chocolate bars - Crunchies, Twirls and scrumptious Wispas
Run to the chocolate, everyone
Playful candy puppies bounding up to play on fabulous sprinkle slides
You land in a pool of yummy sprinkles
And fall into the lollipop lake and relax.

Freya Byrne (9)
Limekilns Primary School, Limekilns

Burger Beach

My visit to Burger Beach is out of this world,
A shark is half-pig, half-burger,
The golden sand doesn't tickle my feet,
Some jellyfish don't sting,
You can eat the lovely bun sand,
The crabs are gherkins,
Amazing turtles are made out of kebabs,
There is a yummy ketchup river,
Cheesy waves,
I want to be here all day!

Louise McKay (9)
Limekilns Primary School, Limekilns

Slime Soup

S *lurp! Slurp!*
L emon-flavoured, slurpy soup
I magine the faces people would make!
M ess everywhere
E ating, chewing, *munch, munch, munch*

S lithering slime
O h no! Out comes a drop
U p and down your spoon goes
P *lop*! That's the last drop!

Rowan Grant (8)
Limekilns Primary School, Limekilns

Shaving Cream Land

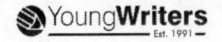

Shaving Cream Land is appearing.
Everyone is sinking
down
down
down.
On the fluffy roller coaster, people are screaming.
The food is frothy and weird.
Swimming feels soft
but remember, you'll sink!
Sniff... *sneeze!* It's up your nose!

Ernie Cruickshank (8)
Limekilns Primary School, Limekilns

Wonderful Waterfall

I saw a waterfall
but it was going up, not down.
It was flowing, blue, shimmering water.
I went to go and touch it
but it changed to different shapes and a sound.
Then the waterfall transformed into a boat!
Whoosh! It sprayed up into the air!

Katie Mia Mulube (8)
Limekilns Primary School, Limekilns

Burgerworld

Giant burgers the size of children
Soft and squishy, that are good to eat
Everything made out of burgers
Turn on the taps and burgers come flying out
Every building in the world is made out of cheeseburgers
When you're hungry, you can eat the world.

Mason Smith (8)
Limekilns Primary School, Limekilns

Cookie Planet

On the wonderful cookie planet
The river drifts past
So chocolatey, so tasty
Mouths water at the sight
The cookie stars shine so bright
Catching your eye every night
The giant cookie sun, hottest of all
Now time for a treat, yum, yum, yum!

Scarlet Donnelly (8)
Limekilns Primary School, Limekilns

Magic Land With Puppies

P uppies are cute
U nder the circus tent they perform
P erfect gymnastics
P laying tig
I n a diamond shape
E verywhere, you can see tightropes and zip lines
S eek out their favourite chew toys.

Lucas Chaplin (8)
Limekilns Primary School, Limekilns

If Dogs Were To Rain From The Sky

All sorts of dogs fall from the sky
More of them can fly
Jack Russells flip and turn all day long
This seems so wrong
Huskies pull a sleigh
Labs and retrievers play
All dogs will stay
We might as well play!

Connor Kevin Brady (8)
Limekilns Primary School, Limekilns

Wacky Burger

Put hot chilli cucumber on the frying pan
Bend flowers with gherkins
Chopped mouse tails for on top
The roll made out of rotten cheese
It is a yummy burger.

Rory Hastings (8)
Limekilns Primary School, Limekilns

Secret Land

S ee the magical, big Secret Land.
E nter the big, bad, crazy bunny's house.
C andy is sweet, sticky, pink and big.
R ainbows are misty, fluffy and very nice.
E nter the pink, misty clouds.
T he big, fluffy unicorn will come to play.

L ollipops are sweet, noisy and sticky.
A baby ladybird loves singing all night.
N oisy, big, blue mice blow bubbles.
D ive into the smooth chocolate river.

Anja Shepherd (8)
Monymusk School, Monymusk

Candyfloss Land

Fluffy blue and pink clouds,
Flying books with little pink wings,
Smell the sweet smell of dancing gummy bears,
Eat the foot of a candyfloss monster, but make sure he is sleeping,
Eat some deliciously sweet candyfloss clouds,
At night, you can see a cookie Saturn,
Chocolate skyscrapers and gummy bear people,
Sail on a chocolate river in a sweetie boat,
Come to Candyfloss Land, you're in for a treat!

Matilda Esson (10)
Monymusk School, Monymusk

My Unicorn

M y unicorn is fluffy
Y ou would like her

U p you go, to see her in the clouds
N ow she lives in Unicorn Land with her friends
I saw a unicorn
C ouldn't help it, I had to take her
O scar, her dad, wanted her to come home
R oseta, her mum, wanted her to go with me!
N ow, how do I get home?

Ashley Nicole Findlay (8)
Monymusk School, Monymusk

Candy Flood In The Desert

It was late at night,
I had just had my tea,
"Your dessert is ready!" Mum yelled,
I started to daydream...
A candy flood in the desert,
my car turned into chocolate,
my scissors snapped in half,
my house turned into a sweetie,
me getting sucked away,
"Nooo...!"
... and I was back in my house!

Jack Strachan (9)
Monymusk School, Monymusk

Candyfloss Cloud

Josh woke up on a thundercloud one day,
My oh my, what would his parents say?
Eating on a cloud of candyfloss.
Making him feel like he was the boss,
An unlimited sweet soda can.
Josh really needed a cold fan.
Flashing and bashing, he couldn't get to sleep,
He had to resort to counting sheep.

Shea Withey (9)
Monymusk School, Monymusk

Mushroom Hotel

The hotel wasn't what I expected
I saw lots of mushrooms
I heard lots of mumbling mushrooms from the other room
They were really noisy.
I couldn't get to sleep
My room was a mess
The TV was on the floor
My bed was upside down
I would never come back again!

Lily Anne Chisholm (8)
Monymusk School, Monymusk

Underwater Mushroom Land

Colourful mushrooms surrounded by fish
Glistening water flowing past the seaweed
Beautiful bubbles pop in the coral reef
Tropical fish play in the sand
Silky seaweed shimmers in the mist
Bright corals are quiet in the reef.

All is calm in Underwater Mushroom Land.

Lily Emma Todd (9)
Monymusk School, Monymusk

Land Of Horrible Things

Bright red blood everywhere,
Cracked shells from snails that have been eaten,
Long, thin worms with sharp teeth crawling out the ground,
Lots of hairy spiders crawling up my back,
Bad bird ate a butterfly's wings!
I don't want to be here anymore.

Reece Donaldson (7)
Monymusk School, Monymusk

Supersonic Magnet

I use my supersonic magnet to take down buildings,
My supersonic magnet is strong, destructive and powerful,
My supersonic magnet makes a noise,
My supersonic magnet goes, *neeee!*
I love my supersonic magnet!

Michael Wood (7)
Monymusk School, Monymusk

Solar System Land

Hear the aliens talking
See the rocket flying past me
Other alien planets, colourful and funny
Aliens singing 'Jingle Bells'
The aliens eat my snack!
I am very hungry
I want to go home now.

Zaysha Brand (8)
Monymusk School, Monymusk

Dinosaur Land

Dinosaurs roaring in the old oak trees.
Huge dinosaurs hurting each other.
I feel the clomping from a dinosaur heading my way,
It's getting louder and louder!
Help! The dinosaurs are here!

Andrew Mitchell (9)
Monymusk School, Monymusk

A Submarine On Saturn

I went to Saturn on a submarine
I saw gold stars twinkling in the light
I ate candy stars
I felt very funny
What would I say when I got home?
I just said I went to Saturn in a submarine.

Abby Ferguson (7)
Monymusk School, Monymusk

Help, I've Shrunk

Help, I'm tiny!
I've fallen in my pencil case
The rubbers are huge!
My dinosaur finger spacers are scary
Rubbers are chasing me
A pencil is poking me in the bum.
Help!

Callum Reid (9)
Monymusk School, Monymusk

Disco On The Moon

Help, too much music!
Green aliens dancing in craters,
Ouch, the disco ball is hurting my eyes!
All there is to eat is cheese.
Where is the pizza?
I'm going home.

Jake Peter Evans (7)
Monymusk School, Monymusk

The Rabbit Hole

T oday, I saw a hole in my classroom I went to take a peek
H ere, I heard robots dancing to funky music, until I fell down
"E ek!" I shouted as I fell down.

R abbits were bouncing
A nd unicorns were singing
B ut then I saw a skeleton
B ut then I saw some bouncy balls
I was laughing at the dragon cat man, then I went plop on the floor
T hen I heard my teacher

"H urry up and wake up!" he said
O h, it was a dream! I was back in the classroom, so yes, it was!
L ee said, "We are doing poems, there have to be rhymes!" Next day...
"E ek!" as I have to deal with math times.

Teagan Sullivan (9)
Newtongrange Primary School, Newtongrange

Kung Fu Aliens

I was walking to karate
one miserable Monday,
I was followed by some aliens,
they wouldn't go away!

Then they punched the sensai,
and forced me to tell
some of the top karate tips,
then they battered me as well!

I ran outside to check
what was happening to me,
when I didn't get the chance,
'cause suddenly, I needed to pee!

I ran into the bathroom,
an alien was there!
When we saw each other,
we just began to stare!

I looked in all the cubicles,
aliens were there too!

Crashing, destroying and wrecking
every single loo!

I just went in the bushes,
then I turned around to see,
then I knew what was
happening to me!

There was an alien invasion!
A flying saucer was on the floor!
Alien karate lessons were in great demand,
there seemed to be more and more!

I ran and ran and ran,
to the supermarket, I fled!
For I feared if I slowed down,
I would end up dead!

There was the poor police lady,
fighting with her bare hands,
and there, in a massive cage,
was my favourite pop star band!

They were looking quite flustered,
'cause the aliens were throwing sticks.

I couldn't believe my eyes,
they'd imprisoned Little Mix!

There was the poor shopping assistant,
tied to a fiery pole,
and the entire police force
was stuck in a great big hole!

As I was shoved into a cage,
I couldn't believe I'd been caught,
I suddenly had a really giant, great,
Big thoughtful thought!

Whatever your regrets,
this is a lesson to you:
never, ever, ever, ever
teach aliens kung fu!

Daisy Fiennes (9)
Newtongrange Primary School, Newtongrange

There's A Dino Playing Fortnite

There's a dino in my room,
it doesn't really fit
and it's playing Fortnite on my Xbox,
how outrageous can it get?

It's already broken the roof
and to be honest, it doesn't really smell good
it roars really loud
and my mum can't get her forty winks!

I walk inside my room
to see what is going on
I immediately back out
to find myself covered in slime
and he can't really hold the controller
it's way too small for him.

For all I know, he nearly got a win
but he got bored
so he went to a different planet
and played a different game.

Flynn Dunlop (9)
Newtongrange Primary School, Newtongrange

The Marshmallows Eating Clouds

One day, I went outside
and up to the hill
I hope this never happens again
really, I don't think it will

I saw some bright white marshmallows
flying into the sky
they were eating all the clouds
I really don't know why

They were gobbling by the hundreds
and ripping them apart
I'm really, really not lying
it nearly broke my heart

So then I got a ladder
from the basement in my house
I soon found out it was a...
sleeping place for a grown-up mouse!

The marshmallows were on the other side
so I had to get past that mouse
I ran back to my house
to get the biggest woodlouse

I placed the woodlouse in the corner
wasn't long before it began to think
then he realised
he was on a big ice rink

So then the mouse went for the woodlouse
so I ran
until I pounced
then, finally, I got to the other side

Suddenly, there was nothing
the marshmallows disappeared
into a puff of smoke
I hope it wasn't a joke

So the marshmallows
were gone in pain
I don't think I will
see them again.

Heather Breeze (9)
Newtongrange Primary School, Newtongrange

Vivienne Likes Horses

Vivienne likes horses, she thinks they are great.
Vivienne likes horses, she doesn't have any mates!

With flowing manes and tails, she thinks they are fantastic,
People stare at her as she admires her horse.
Vivienne likes horses, she thinks they are great.
Vivienne likes horses, she doesn't have any mates!

Standing in a smelly stall, she still thinks they are cool,
People stare at her as she mucks out!
Vivienne likes horses, she thinks they are great,
Vivienne likes horses, she doesn't have any mates!

Vivienne loves to ride them, she likes seeing the world go by,
People stare at her as she goes whizzing by!
Vivienne likes horses, she thinks they are great,
Vivienne likes horses, she doesn't have any mates!

Vivienne also likes grooming them,
They love just being outside!

Caring for a horse is such hard work, but at least she likes horses!
If you want a horse, just read this poem, it gives you some advice!

Vivienne Borkowska (9)
Newtongrange Primary School, Newtongrange

Invite An Elephant To Tea

I will invite an elephant to tea
N ow she is here
V errucas are all over her
I nvite others to tea
"T eatime everyone!"
E llie the elephant is my best friend

A t night, we will enjoy our tea
N ever again will it happen

E llie gets the house soaking
L illy is coming as well
E llie is really funny
P izza is delivered, it is delicious
H am sandwiches are yummy
A mazing tea
N ight-time is near
T ummies are rumbling as the seconds go by

T ea feels warm as a fire
O bviously it was yummy

T ummies are full
E llie the elephant is thankful
A fter, everyone goes home.

Ellie Macfarlane (9)
Newtongrange Primary School, Newtongrange

A Scientist's Dinner

A scientist ate a frog
how disgusting could it get?
Even if he did it again
I wouldn't place a bet

The sliminess and the water
the bitterness and the taste!
It looked so minging
it looked like fish paste!

He must be crazy
to do something like that.
He even tried to eat
a tasty looking cat!

I wouldn't say he was evil
but I wouldn't say he was nice.
His next plan was
to turn children into mice.

When I looked at him
he let out a sudden scream!

I posted it on Snapchat
and then it started a meme.

And then it was digested,
there was one final screech
and that was when I finished
my very funny speech!

Jamie Ramsey (9)
Newtongrange Primary School, Newtongrange

My Boots Don't Stop

M y boots are creeping me out
Y ou can sometimes hear them shout

B anging and opening all day long
O ver the week, I try to be strong
O nly I can feel the storm
T oes are squishy and not warm

C an't be quiet just for a day
A lways loud in my head
N ever-ending, the screaming shreds

T hey always pound
A pair like these need to be found
L ove my boots, but they too go
K nowing this as I make my way home.

Calla Meere (9)
Newtongrange Primary School, Newtongrange

Unicorns Dancing On Rainbows

U nicorns are amazing
N obody will ever see this
I t feels like a dream
C ourse, it was real
O bviously it was not plastic
R unning happily
N apping? There was no such thing
S parkly, shiny horn

D ropping glitter footsteps
A pples dropping from trees
N ever stop being imaginative
C atching a dancing unicorn
I t's so beautiful
N ow it's time to see the final dance
G lorious unicorns dancing.

Jennifer Aitken (9)
Newtongrange Primary School, Newtongrange

Cheerleading Is My Thing Going Down The Street

Cheerleading is my thing
Going down the street
Jumping, catching, all on my feet
Pom-poms are used for fun
Throwing them up high as the sun.

Cheerleading is my thing
Going down the street
High stunts on the front
Feeling scared and excited
Wow, cheer is so #fun!

Cheerleading is so my thing
Going down the street
I can do anything
That a cheerleader can
Back handsprings and front flips!

Cheerleading is my thing
How amazing.
My dream come true!

Kenzie O'Donnell (9)
Newtongrange Primary School, Newtongrange

Bubbles In Space

B eautiful bubbles in space
U nusual bubbles in space
B ubbly bubbles in space
B endy bubbles in space
L ovely bubbles in space
E ntertaining bubbles in space
S oapy bubbles in space

I ncreasing bubbles in space
N aughty bubbles in space

S hiny bubbles in space
P opping bubbles in space
A mazing bubbles in space
C ool bubbles in space
E xciting bubbles in space.

Josh Jenkin (9)
Newtongrange Primary School, Newtongrange

The Random Rhyme Happening

I was surfing in the ocean
There was a lot of commotion
I felt something sticky
It was a hickey from Nicky
It was icky
Nicky, you're quite picky
Yeah Nicky, you're picky

Then I realised I wasn't alone
I was getting licked by a dinosaur!
Actually, it was a spinosaur
I can bet
It was so wet

Then I saw some greedy gremlins in the garbage
They started to starve
I looked at their hair
It was kinda bare.

Calum Higginson (9)
Newtongrange Primary School, Newtongrange

Unicorn And Cheese Disaster!

I am walking out of school,
then I suddenly see,
a unicorn munching on cheese!

Then I realise,
there is a stack of cheese.
I go up and say, "Please!"

The unicorn turns and says,
"No, no, no, not my cheese!"
I say, "No, no, my cheese!"
At this point, I think I have been pushy.

Then I go home.
As soon as I step in my garden,
I hear footsteps,
And someone munching on...
Cheese!

Eilidh Hill (9)
Newtongrange Primary School, Newtongrange

I Am An Alien

I have four arms and luminous skin
I like climbing trees because I have four arms
watch out, I also have luminous blue skin
and, if you look too long, you might go blind!
I have four arms and luminous skin
when I touch lava
I touch it with all four arms
I can go through easily.
I have four arms and luminous skin
it especially comes in handy in taekwondo
and here's a lesson for you:
never drink a potion labelled 'Alien'!

Alex Bell (9)
Newtongrange Primary School, Newtongrange

Visiting A Cookie In Space

A monkey visited a cookie in space
he had an awfully funny face
he was playing hopscotch with a cookie
which was very spooky

The cookie visited a very spooky planet
which was the Cookie Planet!
The aliens gobbled up all the gorgeous cookies
from the spooky cookie cake

The spooky cookie cake
visited the moon
to get a very spooky tune
that was as spooky as the moon!

Thomas Hugh McSweeney (9)
Newtongrange Primary School, Newtongrange

Flying A Cookiesaucer

I will fly my cookiesaucer to

magnificent Mars to see tiny Thomas
then I will go to crispy chocolate Cookie Land
and to my house to eat my tea

I will fly my cookiesaucer to

awesome Fortnite Land
so I can play lots of Fortnite
and have a great time

I will fly my cookiesaucer to

yummy Candy Land
to eat lots of candy
and have a fun time.

Craig Dow (9)
Newtongrange Primary School, Newtongrange

The Cupcake Life

The smart cupcake
went to a party
he dressed very smartly
the joy felt real
I started eating my meal
it wasn't very nice
so I started eating my rice
my cherry fell off
and then I saw a moth
and then we became mates
it felt really great
the rain fell down
it gave me a frown
luckily, I didn't bump into a clown
I love my life!

Lilly Oldham (9)
Newtongrange Primary School, Newtongrange

Space Is Food

S melling the sweetness in Candyland
P owerful cookies fighting
A gingerbread man chasing me
C ookieland is tasty
E ating burgers

I t's a miracle
S inging the cheese song

F ood is everywhere
O nion is smelly
O nion is making my eyes water
D rowning in the cheese hole.

Aila P Waite (9)
Newtongrange Primary School, Newtongrange

Killer Cookies

Killer Cookies landed in space,
then they jumped down and landed on my face.

Killer Cookies will bite your heads,
even if you're asleep in your beds.

Killer Cookies, you're not safe when they're there,
even though they don't have any hair.

Angry and scary is the Killer Cookie,
even though they have a big bahookey!

Aidan Byars (9)
Newtongrange Primary School, Newtongrange

Baking

Baking is inspiring
you can cook anything
baking is fun, baking is cool
anything you bake is delicious
baking is fun, yum, yum, yum
baking, baking, everyone loves baking
baking, caking
chocolate Victoria sponge
baking, everyone knows how to bake
baking is the best
I love baking
baking, baking is over the moon!

Alana Moore (9)
Newtongrange Primary School, Newtongrange

Comic Day!

C omic Lurk, Comic Lurk
O nly I can do the work
M aking up stories
I ncluding some fun
C olourful pictures, then it's done

L ots of ideas, never the same
U nlike the others, which is a shame
R eading out loud and telling others my stories
K apow and pow!

Samuel Smith (9)
Newtongrange Primary School, Newtongrange

The Day The Unicorn Went On The Rainbow

The unicorn saw glitter,
On the rainbow, there was gold,
Clouds above on Unicorn's head, she was looking much fitter,
The unicorns saw math books on top of the sky, that's what she was told,
Slime on the ground,
Bubbles in the sky,
She saw gunk on the mound,
She really didn't know why.

Iyla Croall (9)
Newtongrange Primary School, Newtongrange

Candy Land

Marshmallows are eating sharks
water is turning into candyfloss
Lamborghinis racing
candy canes flossing
Cookie Planet dancing
candy dragons are flying everywhere
dirt turning into chocolate
magic flying in the air
people having fun times.

Jack Smith (9)
Newtongrange Primary School, Newtongrange

The Depths Of My Black Piano

I sat down at my black grand piano
as I wanted to play a tune.
So I opened up my big red book
to find Clair de Lune.

But then I wondered what was wrong
when not a sound was to be heard.
Not the notes of my song,
but the tweet of a little bluebird.

It could've just been me, but did I just hear?
No, I couldn't have... but maybe I did.
I was pretty sure that little bluebird
just told me to open the lid.

I thought I should do so and covered up the keys,
dusted the top and undid the hook.
I opened the lid and looked inside,
but all I saw was a big blue book.

I climbed inside and slid right down,
I got up on my feet and took a look around
and what I saw was a little crazy,
not the blue book, but a plant growing a pound!

Out of the distance came a little gnome
who took me over to a small town.
Everything was peculiar there, such as a little home
with candy windows and candy doors.

The trees there were rather peculiar,
as they were tall, colourful lollipops.
As tall as they did stand,
so brightly coloured they would make you stop.

But then it was time, I really had to go
and I said goodbye to the little gnome.
I retook my steps to the bottom of the slide
and climbed the steps into my home.

Hayley Dunn (11)
Slains Primary School, Collieston

The Homeless Boy

Down in the streets of a dark alleyway,
Stands a forgotten statue made of clay,

With a child weak and slim,
There is no family, no friends for him,

He stands alone for all his days,
And cannot manage to say his Js,

When people walk down the street,
All he asks for is something to eat,

Then, one night when he's asleep,
He is woken up by a sudden beep,

Only to find a lorry filled with hay,
With a kind-looking man shouting, "Hey!"

"Come inside," says the man,
"I have plenty of space in my van.

I have something for you to see."
So in the boy gets, filled with glee.

The man drives him to a place,
Then says to the boy, "Tie your lace!"

So the boy ties his lace,
Not looking at the man's face,

And so they walk miles and miles,
To find two people with two big smiles,

Who they are, the boy does not know,
But the man walks over just to show.

"These are your parents, young child."
The parents say, "Now, we don't want any fuss, we just want you to stay mild."

Off the family goes, all together,
And for the first time in forever and ever,
The boy feels that he will be loved forever.

Stanley Sharp Grasham (11), Fraser Norrie, Brodie Macalister & Ollie Davidson (10)
Slains Primary School, Collieston

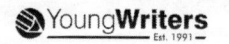

Over My Garden Wall

One sunny day in Aberdeen,
I decided to climb my garden wall,
I gripped and struggled up to the top,
But suddenly began to fall!

My hand grasped the wall,
And I pulled myself up,
I stood on the wall, looking around,
As I looked down, I saw a flying cup!

I felt shivers down my spine,
My heart started to pound,
A hand grabbed me, then pushed me,
I opened my eyes and I was on the ground.

A green monster stood,
Gloopy and blobby, giggling over me,
More and more gathered round,
Ugly and slimy as could be.

I stood up and ran,
Towards the wall,

When I started gripping bricks,
I realised it was much too tall.

I heard something coming,
Making a bristling sound,
It was coming from the bushes...
"Are you listening, Sammy Bound?"

I looked up and saw,
My teacher staring down at me,
"Sorry, Miss Bass,
Seems I was sleeping on my knee!"

Martha Crockett (11)
Slains Primary School, Collieston

A Stream Dream

I look under the rug and what do I see?
A big black hole staring at me!
What could go wrong if I jump under there?
I take my chance
And as I fall, I stare.
Oh, how did this happen? Is this a dream?
I'm standing on an iceberg in the middle of a stream,
Polar bears galore and look, there's more!
I look behind me and what I see is extraordinary,
A mountain! A mountain! It's so tall!
I want to climb it! I hope I don't fall!
Hmm, how do I get there? Let me see...
If I get a ride from a bear, that's quick and easy!
I slide down the iceberg into the stream,
I swim across with a *splish, splash, splosh!*
I jump on a polar bear
And I say, "Over there!"
So we ride and we ride along the tide.
As I trudge up the mountain,

I look around,
What an adventure, what a place to have found.

Maggie Cuthbert (10)
Slains Primary School, Collieston

The Troll Who Stole My Specs

I was once in a land,
A very cold land,
With ice and snow and caves.
I met a troll named Jöll
As I walked along
Near the icy cold waves.

Jöll was smelly and ugly
And hairy and filthy,
I didn't know what to do!
I was wary because he was scary,
But also something new.

I didn't run away, I wish I had,
Because he stole my specs, the naughty lad!
He cackled at me and ran to the sea,
Shouting, "Now I can see the fish for my tea!"

I wouldn't have minded,
But they were my favourite pair

And now they're all the way over there,
With a troll named Jöll.

Esme Macalister (9)
Slains Primary School, Collieston

Plastic

"Plastic, plastic, a wonderful thing!"
That's what they all said when they made that ring.
A few years of fun
it was still on the run
until people started to realise
that plastic should be penalised.
Many animals have started to lose their lives
along with lots and lots of beehives.
Sea creatures die all over the place
due to all our plastic waste.

If we don't do something fast
then the human race won't last.

Grace Bagshaw (11) & Piper Róisín Burrows
Slains Primary School, Collieston

My Quad

My quad is fast, my quad is cool,
My dad helped me fix it with his tools.

When I go fast, I leave a muddy trail
And figure-of-eights around a bale.

If you see me on the track,
I'll race you to the gate and back.

I press down on the throttle,
My quad goes so fast, but I never topple.

Ollie Davidson (10)
Slains Primary School, Collieston

The Gruffalo Goalie

This all begins in this one place out of all
Cookieville Avenue is where this game takes its toll
We sit with creatures big and small.

Fans are piling in
as the teams take their lines.
We hear the music start
and we know it is finally time.

The teams come out and all shake hands
the goat referee calls over the captains.
He says, "Right mate, call slugs or snails."
Bessi says, "I'll call slugs."
Fonaldo says, "Bet it is snails."

Fonaldo wins the toss
but insists Bessi's team take the kick-off.
Finally, after everything that has happened
the teams are underway
I think this will be a very special day.

Five minutes in and our team are down by one.
The manager says to his assistant,

"I think it's time for a change.
Call over our number one goalie,
he might just change the game."

The goat ref blows his whistle
the change is finally happening
not the one we were expecting
but the manager starts clapping.

Here he comes, our new January signing
big orange eyes and a wart at the end of his nose
purple spikes down his back
also, pointy nails for his toes.

Forty-five minutes into the game and it's half-time.
Our manager says, "Mosquito Mangos, anyone?"
"That's lovely," says the Gruffalo
He may have committed a crime.

The teams are out for the second half
we really have not been the best
but sixty-five minutes in and our striker pops it in the net!
Our striker runs for the ball

places it in the whipped cream centre circle.

The Gruffalo Goalie saves a shot
he gets up for the second
and pushes it inches wide.
Ninety minutes have passed
two minutes added on.
The ball comes back to our Gruffalo Goalie
and with no attempt at all, he scores a goal!

The game is finished
and we finally win a game.
We go home in our car.
"The Gruffalo Goalie," we say,
"What a star!"

Lewis Austin (11)
St Dominic's Primary School, Airdrie

How Not To Brush A Monster's Teeth

Oh no! It's that time again
The monsters' teeth are green again
So I pick up the toothbrush
Put it in a giant pineapple
I start brushing the monsters' teeth.

He growls and snarls and starts to bite
He scratches and hits and starts a fight
I hit him hard, but he pushes me back
Oh, what a night this will be.

In the morning, I try it again
But the same thing happens all over again
He growls and snarls and starts a fight
What will I do now?

The next day, he comes with teeth ever so bright
No more scratching or hitting or anymore fights
But how did this happen? How has it come?
Whoever it was is as good as none.

Cara Sweeney (11)
St Dominic's Primary School, Airdrie

My Brother Turned Into A Whale

This summer was a very crazy summer,
me and my brother were out on the beach,
we went to the nearest bar to drink something,
we went back out to the beach for a swim,
but it felt very weird,
a big shark jumped out of the water and bit my brother,
then the shark disappeared,
he got bit on the leg, it looked very bad,
we swam back, he was okay.
His leg was turning blue,
we went back home.
The next day, he got bluer and bluer,
he even got bigger,
he had difficulty breathing.
Next day, he was a fish,
but his head was still there.
I went to the pet shop and bought an aquarium.
One day passed, I was sleeping on the ground,
and the whole house was destroyed!

I rushed to the beach and I saw a whale,
on a broken chair with sunglasses.
The whale fell in the water,
the waves pushed me in the water,
then I got eaten by the whale.
When I was inside the whale,
I found out that it was my brother.
I was stuck inside my brother's stomach,
I never got out of my brother's stomach,
until that day his stomach opened up and I got out!
But when I got out, I turned into a whale too,
then we lived happily ever after!

Olaf Filipiak (11)
St Dominic's Primary School, Airdrie

Bananaland

In Bananaland, it's like no other
We only have one rule
We just play all day
So, we have banana history
Just now we are learning about
Banana War Two
Last year, we were learning about
The Big Banana Ship.

Well, we only have one rule
Before I tell you...
Just joking, it's: Have fun!
And have parties every Monday and Tuesday
Wednesday, Thursday
Wait, don't forget Friday!
Oh dear, I forgot to tell you
About Bananaday.

When it is Bananaday
We get to see a
Banana legend.
I like Cristiano Banono

I saw him once
That was
The best time of my life.

No, no, I've got to go
It's my bedtime
Whoever is reading this
Say 'banana' three times
And you can visit Bananaland.

Michael Fitzpatrick (11)
St Dominic's Primary School, Airdrie

Flying A Dragon Into Space

One day, we wanted to go up and up, higher than anyone else,
so I jumped on my loyal friend.
His name was Toothless,
and he was a dragon.
We took off so fast,
high into the gorgeous sky.

There we were, up so high,
having so much fun,
flying up in the sky,
feeling all the fluffy clouds,
racing other people,
and feeling all the powerful wind,
as we zoomed through the sky.

But we wanted to go higher,
so we did,
higher and higher,
until, suddenly, we were there,
up so high we could see the whole Earth,

and all the beautiful stars,
as if we could hear them,
twinkling in the air.

Alicja Matys (11)
St Dominic's Primary School, Airdrie

The Ocean Under The Sea

Down I go, what do I see?
Is that someone down there
waving at me?

My heart is pounding
I feel the breeze
look at that!
Is it an ocean under the sea?

Oh, it's so beautiful
I'm amazed at what I see
I love it, it's my ocean under the sea.

Is that a mermaid
playing with tea?
I really want to join her
let me go and see.

I saw her playing with shellfish
and they were being very selfish
I go and ask her if I can play
but she swims away
I felt really sad, I just wanted some tea

but I have to go now
back above the sea.

Siobhan McGowan (11)
St Dominic's Primary School, Airdrie

The Man With A Candyfloss Beard

Once upon a time, when he was young
The man with his bushy pink beard
came to town.
He came with his family who were all so weird
but him, he had a candyfloss beard.

He walked through the streets of Candy Cane Lane
then out of the blue, it began to rain.
Growing, growing, his beard flooded the town
everyone's feet were getting stuck down.
The more it rained
the more his beard grew.

Who knows where he is now?
I don't know
because all the neighbours paid him to go.
He went on walking with his beard on his back
and a shrinking spell placed nicely in his sack.

Taylor John McLaughlan (11)
St Dominic's Primary School, Airdrie

Cupcake Island In Dessert Fantasy

In Cupcake Island, whatever you see
may turn into sponge.
Dessert Island is where it is.
"Chocolate rivers
that's where I swim."

"Who said that?"
"Me, the man who looks forwards and never backwards.
I live in a chilli, it's very cold."
"That's not possible."
"Oh yes it is.
It's your imagination."

He is a gingerbread man
with sprinkles as hair
and gummies as shoes.
He has a candyfloss beard,
chocolate chips for eyes
and when he cries, there are sprinkles
in his eyes.

Marvin Daly (11)
St Dominic's Primary School, Airdrie

The Mushroom Monster

Candyland, beautiful and magical
Candy and sweets, that's my life
Life must be wonderful
But not now with a monster in town
What's his name? The mushroom monster!
He's tall and scaly and very, very ferocious!
Please help... this life's a misery.

My house is a mushroom, so he ate it
He's eaten the candyfloss clouds
The candy cane trees too
What next?
Oh no, the gingerbread house! It's gone!
He's eating way too many mushrooms!
He's going to turn into one!
Oh no! He's the mushroom monster!

Shea McCarthy (11)
St Dominic's Primary School, Airdrie

Clowns In Town

Clowns in town
are a pain at first
but it will get worse
just wait and see.

Ten-foot clowns standing on houses
some running around
with kids laughing at them.

Having a BBQ it smells nice
the fresh air
up in the sky, the birds
chirping like they don't care.

Little clowns running
around with fish
some clowns honking their horns.

A clown took my car downtown
he turned stone cold
and crashed into a tree.

Go home to Clown Town now
you have made a mess of our town.

Chiara Reid (11)
St Dominic's Primary School, Airdrie

My Family Are Monkeys

My name is Aiden and I am a boy
but my brother, my mum and my dad are monkeys!
Some call me Monkey Boy
but I think I'm Monkey Man!
It's not easy being a human and having a monkey family.
It hurts when my monkey mum washes my hair as well.
My family live in the jungle,
so all I smell is animal poo.
I don't care what anyone says
my monkey mum makes the best bug pie!
She takes the bugs from me and my brother's hair
a little secret: I love pizza.

Aiden Armstrong (11)
St Dominic's Primary School, Airdrie

Tsunami Makes Friends

A tsunami turned into a human
He saw beaches made out of chocolate coins
Leaning tower of candyfloss
When he got off the chocolate coins
The tsunami felt concrete and grass

Tsunami saw an underwater volcano
The tsunami made a friend, it was the volcano
The volcano called Liam
Tsunami and Liam went out to the sea
They were best friends forever.

Aiden McGleish (11)
St Dominic's Primary School, Airdrie

My Brother's A Genie

My brother is a genie
a pink and red one, in fact
because he got sacked
from a strawberry shack
located in Shark Park.

He gets me what I want
he got me a pet ant
and even an elephant.

Overall we like to fall
off of toaster coaster
my mum and dad are very tall
and I am small
overall, my family is crazy
and very lazy.

Fraser Courtney (11)
St Dominic's Primary School, Airdrie

Having A Picnic

Jack was sitting on the house,
then he walked to the sun.
He grabbed his things
and was on his way.
It took him one second.
When he got there, he stopped at the station.
He walked on the sun,
he put his food on his blanket.
As he was sitting, he saw the planet
and the black of space.
An alien took his sandwich
and they became friends.

Jack Crawford (11)
St Dominic's Primary School, Airdrie

My Day With A Unicorn

When I woke up,
I found myself next to a unicorn,
She had pink, yellow and purple hair,
That got into my breakfast,
Yuck!
She had a pointy horn at the top of her head,
That made a hole in my ceiling,
Oi!
She smelt of fresh flowers,
That were fresh that day.
Her home was a rainbow,
And she was taking me there just then,
That was exciting!
We went on a cloud,
That was light and fluffy,
It was like a bus with no roof.
Five minutes later and we had arrived,
The ground was like a large, flat rainbow,
Some of the houses were made of non-melting chocolate, gingerbread, clouds or sweets.
The unicorn's house was made out of clouds,

When I went inside, I found out that everything was made of clouds.
As soon as we had tea,
Which was spaghetti and clouds,
I went back home, feeling sad without the unicorn.
That night, all I dreamed about was the unicorn.
When the morning came, I found the unicorn lying beside me.

Neve Thompson (9)
Westerton Primary School, Bearsden

Tea With A Bird

T ea and cakes all on a saucer,
E very bird gathers around a small, circular table,
A nd then I see a little robin, all soft and fluffy.

W hen I walk over to the little table, I sit down and the robin flies over,
I am so surprised as the robin begins to chat,
T he robin keeps on talking while some bluebirds serve us delicious cakes,
H ungry birds line up for some seeds as a crow hands them out.

A t the same time, the robin is pulling me away.

"B ut where are we going?" I ask as I walk into a bush,
I see flowers, trees and a little purple leaf,
R ed flowers are all over the place with a tree of robins high up above,
D ays go by and I live in the tall tree with all the robins.

Hayley Jessie Speedie (9)
Westerton Primary School, Bearsden

Center Parcs Wild Chocolate Pool!

C hocolate pools are the best, free chocolate and swimming in it!
H ollow rocks on the walls and chocolate dogs stuck to them!
O tters diving in with their mouths wide open. "Oh, I wonder how animals got in here!" I cry.
C hatting and splashing is all I hear, but...
O ne more sound appears... the sound of dogs barking!
L arge chocolate waves splash on people and animals, but bats hang inside the pitch-black cave.
A nyone can scare the bats... they are as nervous as deer!
T errific fun all around, eating, swimming and playing with animals.
E xcited shouting and dogs howling... "Oh, I wish I could live here!" I cry in excitement.

Aimee Tabram (9)
Westerton Primary School, Bearsden

Having Lunch With An Octopus!

Have you heard
that I'm having lunch with the most absurd person?
He has pink and blue spots
he's covered in dots.
He's an octopus!
My house is made of chocolate cake
so when it's hot, my house starts to bake
so I get covered in delicious tasting chocolate!
When he first came
I said in shame
"I only have pepperoni pizza."
"Is it from Domino's?" he replied.
"No," I sighed.
"I like your shirt
it has some dirt!"
We munched
and we crunched
all our way through lunch.

When we were finished
we ate mango
whilst doing the tango!
What fun
dancing in the setting sun.

Juliette Hay (9)
Westerton Primary School, Bearsden

The Shop That Sells Unusual And Magnificent Things

Here's David's shopping list
for the shop that sells
unusual and magnificent things...

A jar of fire,
to defeat the nasty dragon on my roof.
A potion of youth,
to make my 1,000-year-old granny young again.
A magic wand,
for turning my annoying brother into a dirty frog.
A mouldy potato,
for the annual mouldy and disgusting food competition.
A giant chocolate bar,
because, well, uh, um... everybody likes chocolate!
A new pet flying donkey,
because the old one ran away.
A new professional cook,

to cook my new favourite food, grass pie!
And, last item, a sword,
to replace the old kitchen knife.

Murray Rasmussen (9)
Westerton Primary School, Bearsden

Underwater BBQ!

U nder horrible saltwater
N ow time to try and cook a squid
D own underwater is the worst for barbecues
E ating with a shark is a bad idea
R unning water down my bun for my hot dog
W atery flood floating around in the water
A fter my wet hot dog, I can hear laughing because of the shark
T ime to play with the sharks, whales and fish
E ndless fish floating past, making the hot dogs dance
R ainbow fish flying by

B eautiful pink sharks dancing through the day
B urger buns running while doing the worm
Q ueueing hot dogs ready to get splashed.

Ethan MacPherson (9)
Westerton Primary School, Bearsden

The Forest Of Candy

The Forest of Candy is far away,
From the crazy modern world today,
But you must not brag when I take you there,
Right into the dragon's lair,
Because if you do...
Well, I just wouldn't want to be you!
So when we get there, you will see,
Just what a wonderful place it is to be,
It's got,
Candy cars that run on rainbow juice,
And crazy gummy bears that just won't stay put,
Rolling wagon wheels are just the worst,
They look like they've been cursed!
Some crazy foes,
That just won't blow their nose!
And finally it's the end,
We just went round,
The final bend.

Phoebe Cuthbertson (9)
Westerton Primary School, Bearsden

Small As An Ant

Bang! I was so tiny,
everything was so bright and shiny.
I had turned into an ant,
And I'd lost my pants!
I went to a hole
and there popped out a mole.
She looked so cool
but she was running late for school.
She ran past me,
"Wow, she's fast!"
The next day, I made my bed
and went to my friend Ted.
He looked around.
"Hey! Down here!" I said.
"Where?" Ted said.
Was he blind?
"Hey, I heard that!"
"Argh! A bat!"
I pointed,
he looked around and I was gone,
dun dun dun!

Suzie Rooney (9)
Westerton Primary School, Bearsden

Candy Land!

When I go to Candy Land,
I see sweets as soft as sand.
I see a candy cane as small as a drain,
there are sugar mice and a tiny piece of rice.

There's a scary sweet called liquorice,
and false teeth from a daisy's leaf.
There're green gerbils playing on hurdles,
in a pit full of turtles.
Now I am done playing in the sun,
now all I have to do is have more fun,
with a piece of gum!

I want to have some party fun,
and dance away in the sun.
Now it's night and day is done,
I need to say bye to candy fun!

Tanisha Thapar (9)
Westerton Primary School, Bearsden

My Trip To The Concert

One day, I went to a concert
and it seemed like a normal concert
until I went inside...
My ears were bleeding
with people screaming
and Irish music filling the room.
I was very confused
until I saw a line of dancing leprechauns!
I was wishing that I was in a dream
until someone offered me some ice cream.
They asked for me to go on stage
and I said, "I will do what they say."
So I went and got on stage
I was very embarrassed by people laughing
so thought it was time to just go home
where I was safe.

Stuart MacKenzie (9)
Westerton Primary School, Bearsden

Candyland

One day, I woke up in Candyland,
I looked out to see who was about,
No one was there,
So I went downstairs and found a living gingerbread man,
He looked like he was eating ice cream,
I ran outside to find that every house was gingerbread,
The trees were cotton candy and rocks were M&M's,
Everything was delicious and so sweet,
I saw a gummy bear chewing some gum, running across the street,
Making a cool beat.
I loved staying in Candyland,
Because everything was sweet,
I just hoped it was not a dream.

Ava Mamie Wilson (10)
Westerton Primary School, Bearsden

Gerbils On The Moon

When I went to the moon,
I saw gerbils everywhere.
I started to look at them and they were...
Soft to stroke,
Cute when I looked,
Squeaky when I listened,
As green as grass (which was unusual),
But it wasn't just the gerbils that were green,
It was the trees, bushes and plants as well.

I had a taste of sugar mice,
With my packed lunch, which was nice.
I saw a UFO,
It was green, though.

After all of this, I got a fright,
And went home in my spaceship,
But I enjoyed my trip.

Isobel Collingwood (9)
Westerton Primary School, Bearsden

Blowing Bubbles On The Moon

B ubbles going into moon craters,
L oud music coming out of moon craters,
O range bubbles blowing out of the tub,
W ild animals popping out of the craters,
I n goes the stick,
N othing can spoil the fun,
G oing down the holes.

B lowing bubbles every second,
U p go the bubbles,
B ubbles, bubbles,
B lowing everywhere,
L aughing, down they go,
E njoying blowing bubbles,
S miling all the time.

Blair Auld (9)
Westerton Primary School, Bearsden

House On A Rainbow

Last night, my house got put on a rainbow,
There were dancing bananas, llamas and unicorns!
Cupcakes were pouring out a big rainbow machine,
I was living in a wonderland!

My favourite music was playing,
I couldn't wish for anything else.
The wind was blowing and glitter was falling down the sides.
I saw my friends playing down below,
I was happy, I was very happy,
In fact, I could not feel my toes!
I went to bed, but woke up on land,
I felt sad, but I got a unicorn to keep!

Sophie Smith (9)
Westerton Primary School, Bearsden

Having Breakfast With A Gummy Bear

I was somehow having breakfast with a gummy bear
whose breath was swirling through the air.
She had hair that was purple and pink
and pens that were smothered in ink.

For breakfast, we had ice cream
and she screamed and screamed and screamed
"Brain freeze!"

She squeezed through the door
then jumped on the floor.
The floor jiggled like crazy!

That night, she wriggled and wriggled in bed
and bumped her head
then cried with her teddy, Ted.

Anna McGregor (9)
Westerton Primary School, Bearsden

Sweetie Land!

S our candy falling above you.
W onderful white sweets surrounding you.
E pic gummy bears playing games.
E pic candy houses.
T en gummy bears walking around me.
I t all made sense
E ver since I was in Sweetie Land.

L ettuce-shaped leaves sprouting up from the ground.
A ll around, gummy bears were talking and laughing.
N ever would I leave this new world.
D ancing and singing, I joined in with the fun.

Arya Chakraborty (8)
Westerton Primary School, Bearsden

Surfing On A Shark

When I woke up, I was surfing on a shark
I could hear splashing and the gnashing of teeth
Unicorns galloping with horns as long as me!
I could see fish with tails like mermaids'
Dolphins splashing beside me
I reached out and touched the unicorn
But then my hair was made of ice cream!
I could smell rainbows and unicorn poop
I wasn't looking forwards...
And crashed into a rock!
I woke up in shock
But the next night, I dreamed of...
Goblins at Laser Planet!

Euan Mitchell (10)
Westerton Primary School, Bearsden

Cookie Festival

I jumped on a cookie crumb,
In a flash, I was in Cookie Land...

Monkeys drove cars of sushi,
Homes of burgers with fry garages,
Monkeys tap-dancing to music,
Monkeys with bow ties and top hats and jackets!

The mayor of Cookie Land was coming -
The mayor was pushing the grand cookie!
After, we had the cookie cake with cookie ice cream.
I ate the cookie cake with cookie sauce.

Then I went home and had spaghetti for dinner.

James Finch Mathew (9)
Westerton Primary School, Bearsden

Wild Party With Gerbils

W ild gerbils on the run,
I n the world of party fun,
L aughing through, all the way,
D ancing and laughing always,

G oing on a ride to thrill,
E nergetic, unable to contain the fun,
R eally happy when they arrive,
B reaking everything they see,
I ce cream everywhere,
L icking from the floor,
S inging gerbils every day!

Lulu Alfayez (9)
Westerton Primary School, Bearsden

Me And The Dancing Monkeys

You might think monkeys are messy
but not here, no, no, they are very tidy.

I woke up here on a beach
nothing but monkeys dancing and a DJ monkey.

I found it hard to believe the monkeys, even the DJ monkey
so guess what I did?

I went and danced, but then heard a voice
it was my mum's voice...

Then I woke up
it was all just a dream...

Annie Miller (9)
Westerton Primary School, Bearsden

Cheese Playing Guitars

Once, in the middle of the night, I got woken up by loud music,
And you'll never guess what it was.
Cheese playing guitars!
It was made of so much fun,
Sometimes when it got too loud, I screamed, "Cringe attack!"
Well, you might say, "How is that true?"
Well, let me tell you.
So I left my house and when I saw them, I said, "Wow!"

Skye Dick (9)
Westerton Primary School, Bearsden

Cake Party

It's a nice sunny day
Bunnies go out to play
Cakes everywhere!
"Wow!" I say
There is a big cake drum
And my tum is saying
"Eat all the cake!
Don't put it to waste!"
A bunny is wearing a hat
That looks like a cat
It always makes me laugh
There is cake everywhere
It is a cake party!

Sophie Collins (9)
Westerton Primary School, Bearsden

Bonkers Banana Birthday Party

Bouncing bananas everywhere
Disco lights in my face
Bouncing around, eating cake
Smelling fresh cake getting baked
In the neat banana lake
Banana bow ties, yellow and green
Streaming round the air
Bananas dancing to Banana Bob
Goodnight, bananas!
I've had a blast
See you next week!

Anna White Wilson (10)
Westerton Primary School, Bearsden

Mystical, Magical Beach

Waking up on the soft sand,
seeing a rainbow bird, red sharks,
little gold flying fish,
and big blue bears.
Behind a rock is a mini jungle,
there are bones and cheetahs,
and magical flyers,
now back at the beach,
it is all gone!

Lij McCulloch (9)
Westerton Primary School, Bearsden

Shark King

When I woke up on Sunday morning
I was a shark
but not just any shark...

I was king of the sharks
and I lived in an ark
with sharks everywhere!

I slept on a coral bed
and when I woke up
I was a human!

Oscar Murray Wilson (10)
Westerton Primary School, Bearsden

Young Writers Information

We hope you have enjoyed reading this book – and that you will continue to in the coming years.

If you're a young writer who enjoys reading and creative writing, or the parent of an enthusiastic poet or story writer, do visit our website www.youngwriters.co.uk. Here you will find free competitions, workshops and games, as well as recommended reads, a poetry glossary and our blog. There's lots to keep budding writers motivated to write!

If you would like to order further copies of this book, or any of our other titles, then please give us a call or visit www.youngwriters.co.uk.

Young Writers
Remus House
Coltsfoot Drive
Peterborough
PE2 9BF
(01733) 890066
info@youngwriters.co.uk

Join in the conversation!
Tips, news, giveaways and much more!

YoungWritersUK @YoungWritersCW